GEORGE WASHINGTON WILSON
AND
ROYAL DEESIDE

Published by AUL Publishing, Queen Mother Library,
Meston Walk, Aberdeen AB9 2UE (tel. 01224 272594).

ISBN 1 874078 06 8 (previous ISBN 0 9507909 7 4)

Printed by Fretwell Print And Design, Healey Works, Goulbourne Street, Keighley, Yorkshire

George Washington Wilson
and

ROYAL DEESIDE

JOHN S. SMITH
MA, PHD, FSA Scot

Photographs from the George Washington Wilson Collection

Edited for the Library Committee of the University of Aberdeen by
Peter L. Payne

Editor's Preface

George Washington Wilson by Sir George Reid RSA
(reproduced by kind permission of Aberdeen Art Gallery & Museums)

The University of Aberdeen's collection of George Washington Wilson photographic negatives has justifiably been described as a "most valuable storehouse of topographical material." It is more than that: these negatives, which date from c. 1870 to 1908, portray many facets of the infinite variety of late Victorian and Edwardian life not only in Britain but in several places overseas. The collection, consisting of no less than 45,000 glass negatives, comprises what was essentially the stock in trade of George Washington Wilson & Co. when that company went into liquidation in 1908. Started in the early 'fifties by George Washington Wilson, a portrait miniaturist who quickly perceived the commercial potentialities of photography and who pioneered both new methods utilising the wet collodion process (particularly "instantaneous" photography) and remarkably efficient mass production techniques, Wilson combined an artistic sensitivity with great entrepreneurial flair. The firm he created became probably the most important commercial enterprise of its kind in the closing decades of the nineteenth century, enjoying a greater reputation and a larger sale than its principal rivals, the firms established by James Valentine, Francis Firth, William Lawrence and Francis Bedford.

The University's collection has been dipped into to illustrate several important studies in economic and social history and George Washington Wilson himself and the firm that he founded has been the subject of a fascinating monograph by Roger Taylor, George Washington Wilson: Artist and Photographer, 1823–1893 *(Aberdeen University Press, 1981), but the riches of this magnificent collection remain largely unexploited. It is the object of this series of booklets to reveal the great historical and sociological value of the Wilson collection and to provide a fresh viewpoint on the life and landscape of late Victorian Britain and those parts of the world "covered" by the photographers employed by the firm.*

This contribution to the series has been prepared by John S. Smith, author of the first title in this series, George Washington Wilson's Aberdeen. *John Smith's abiding interest in Deeside, which has formed the subject of numerous, highly successful extra-mural lectures over the past few years, will be readily apparent both from his choice of photographs and his informative text and captions. For comparative purposes, a number of contemporary views have been included in this booklet; these were taken by Mr. Jim Livingstone, to whom we would like to express our thanks.*

Peter L. Payne

Introduction

THE photographs presented in this booklet recall Deeside in late Victorian and Edwardian times when the Deeside Railway and connecting coaches and omnibuses brought many visitors, including representatives of the aristocracy of Europe, to the mansions and hunting lodges of middle and upper Deeside. The recreational role of Deeside and the royal interest, already firmly established by the medieval period, were enhanced by Queen Victoria and the Prince Consort whose acquisition of Balmoral in 1848 placed the valley firmly on the international map. The Deeside landowners, such as the Duke of Fife in Mar and William Cunliffe Brooks in Glen Tanar, invested in new shooting lodges and improved deer stock, while the range of services offered in the villages expanded in sympathy with the greatly enlarged temporary summer and autumn visitor populations. The health-giving qualities of mountain air and dramatic scenery encouraged many families to rent property on Deeside annually for their summer breaks. The same combination of laird and royal interest furthered the evolution of the Braemar Royal Highland Society, while over the same period the evidence of the old subsistence style of agriculture in the landscape was gradually being effaced. In lower Deeside, the photographer catches the beginnings of *rus in urbe,* or suburbia, both in Cults and Banchory. These settlements were linked by rail to Aberdeen in the early 'fifties, while by the 1890's, Cults was served by a suburban railway or 'subbie' service whose efficiency and timing by all accounts was superb. Favourite photographic sites such as the east end of Banchory High Street, record the changing shopping facade and improved frontages of an expanding settlement, albeit with far from perfect road and pavement surfaces.

The selection of photographs here presented thus encapsulates a Deeside which is just beyond living memory, and one whose growth and investment inputs were rather more dramatic than at present. A number of contemporary views are included to illustrate the immense range in degree of change in the Deeside scene over the last ninety years. Dating of the photographs has been achieved, where possible, initially through the appearance or extension phases of major buildings, particularly churches, and through public buildings and commemorative fountains which can be associated directly with Queen Victoria's Golden Jubilee (1887) and Diamond Jubilee (1897). In the street scenes, local guidebook advertisements and the appearance of specific shops and shop-owners have helped. In at least one case, the clarity of the George Washington Wilson photographs enable dating through the announcement of an important national event on a newsagent's board. On several occasions, a combination of these methods suggests that the photographer took the shot immediately after the building or fountain had been inaugurated. In suburban scenes, the appearance of certain mansions in the annual Aberdeen *Post Office Directory* provides a guide to the date.

Bibliography

James Brown, *The New Deeside Guide* (Aberdeen, 1860 edition).
R. W. Clark, *Balmoral — Queen Victoria's Highland Home* (London, 1981).
A. I. McConnochie, *Queen Victoria's Highland Home and Vicinity* (Aberdeen, 1897).
A. I. McConnochie, *Views of Royal Deeside,* (Aberdeen, 1905).
John Mackintosh, *History of the Valley of the Dee,* (Aberdeen, 1895).

Mar Lodge (1898), the Stag Ballroom and Home farm from the vicinity of Mildarroch.

Inverey, Mar Lodge and the Linn of Dee

Historically, the Lands of Inverey and Glen Ey belonged to the Farquharson's of Inverey, centred on their rudimentary fortified house whose foundations still survive below Meikle Inverey. The best known member of the family was John Farquharson, the Black Colonel who was a staunch Jacobite and supporter of Viscount Dundee. In 1689, the Black Colonel burnt Braemar Castle to prevent its use by General Mackay and the Government troops. In retaliation, Inverey Castle was destroyed and its laird eventually sought refuge in nearby Glen Ey, hiding out on a rocky gorge ledge still known as "The Colonel's Bed". John Farquharson ultimately secured a pardon, and died peacefully in his bed in 1698. His heir, Peter Farquharson, came out for the Jacobites in 1715, but after Sheriffmuir, escaped to Holland. Although the Inverey Farquharson's remained loyal to the Stuart cause, they retained their estates until the 1780's, when they were purchased by the Earl of Fife. His descendents were to purchase the Dalmore (Mar Lodge) lands and also Balmoral, to augment their other Scottish holdings in Moray and Banffshire. The twin villages of Inverey More (Meikle or Muckle Inverey) to the east of the Ey, and Inverey Beg (Little Inverey) to the west, straggling in a vaguely linear fashion astride the Ey, claimed two schools into the twentieth century, and the village population with its smallholdings was swollen by the late nineteenth century Glen Ey clearances. Writing in 1895 (but probably recalling a summer visit made in 1893), Macintosh notes that "in Muckle Inverey there are twelve houses, most of them recently erected and slated, but three or four of the old thatched ones still remain". He adds that "there is about the same number of houses in Little Inverey, five of which are thatched, some of the others in ruins, and four or five are slated. In the vicinity of the straggling hamlets on either side of the waters of the Ey, there is a considerable space of cultivated ground". The photographs of Inverey which follow are approximately synchronous with Macintosh's description, and by displaying the mixture of old and new suggest the beginnings of decay in smallholding agriculture which is totally complete today. The Duke of Fife's sporting interests in the area were initiated by the building of "Old Mar Lodge", a box-like building on the site of the present Mar Lodge. This was followed by Corriemulzie and its associated buildings on the south side of the valley when Old Mar Lodge was damaged by the 1829 flood and, after the Corriemulzie fire, the construction of the present Mar Lodge, completed in 1898.

Corriemulzie Bridge and the Falls of Corriemulzie
This locality was one much beloved by the Victorians, especially those resident in the 'New' Mar Lodge, and the gorge below the falls was improved by the introduction of a variety of tree species, including a Copper Beech. Although the bridge which is illustrated here was 'topped' by a more modern structure in 1983, the character of the view was retained.

The Bridge at the Linn of Dee

This bridge was erected by the fifth Earl of Fife and opened by H.M. Queen Victoria and the Prince Consort on 8th September, 1857. A plaque records the event on the upstream side of the bridge. This superbly built granite bridge replaced an earlier wooden structure which figures in the *Illustrated London News* of 1848, the year of Queen Victoria's first visit to Deeside. The photograph shows the Fife coat of arms (now weathered away) with the twin mottoes *"Deo juvante deus juvat"* and *"Virtute et opera"*, set within a recess on the downstream side. The same shield appears again in Braemar at the main entrance to the Princess Royal and Duke of Fife Memorial Park and above the entrance porch to the Fife Arms Hotel. Queen Victoria's *Journal* records the opening of the Linn Bridge with the road decorated by a triumphal archway and lined with Duff Highlanders – the Duke's estate workers. As the pipers played, the company "drank in whisky – prosperity to the bridge". Linn O' Dee cottage, which stands on the south side of the bridge, was built as a small hunting lodge for the Duke of Fife, and retains its now converted deer larder set against the east gable. The stone foundations which survive in forest clearings on either side of the Linn road between the bridge and Inverey are tangible evidence of Macintosh's statement that in summer 1893, he observed "good crops of corn, potatoes and turnips" on the terraces on the south side of the Dee.

The 'New' Mar Lodge at Corriemulzie

This lodge, built by the Earl of Fife on the southern side of the Dee on a bench below the crags of Creag an Fhithuch, developed out of the largely wooden building known as Corriemulzie Cottage, following damage to Mar Lodge after the 1829 flood. Much of the complex burnt down in summer, 1895, and was replaced by the present Tudor-style Mar Lodge which was built on the site of the first Mar Lodge for the Duke of Fife and the Princess Royal. Little remains of the buildings featured in this photograph save for the dairy, an ice-house, and, to the east of the old Corriemulzie Reservoir, the foundations of the laundry and extensive tipped material. The reservoir provided power for the lodge.

Meikle Inverey looking towards the present Mar Lodge and Home Farm Steadings

This photograph, taken in the first few years of the twentieth century, reveals Inverey largely as it is today, although the wooden fences and well-maintained steadings and corn ricks demonstrate that the lands were still cultivated. The T-plan cottage in the centre foreground was originally Inverey School, while just beyond stands Thistle Cottage, once the home of well-kent Deeside personality Maggie Gruer, who died in 1939. Behind Thistle Cottage stand Hawthorn Cottage and Bourtree. At least one of the two cottages subsequently abandoned or converted to barns appears to be inhabited. The stone enclosures on the southern side of the road represent the remains of the cottages and outhouses which in the nineteenth century lined both sides of the road. Although there are signs of felling on the hill in the background, the relatively dense pine cover pre-dates the war-time demands of the twentieth century.

Little Inverey looking west towards Glen Derry
This view, which may date from the 1870's, is taken from a site just to the west of the present Inverey Outdoor Centre (the old Roman Catholic School). In the foreground are signs of old kitchen garden cultivation terraces (just to the left of the photographer's assistant), while hay ricks, dykes and stone clearance heaps abound in the middle ground. The state of some of the outbuildings suggest that a measure of depopulation of the active population had already begun, although on the roadside near the pony and chaise, a pile of snedded and barked timber awaits milling.

Comparative view in 1984 from the same viewpoint
This reveals that the two substantial cottages remain, renovated and re-roofed, but that the majority of the other features survive only in their foundations. Note, for example, the foundation of the building at the road bend, just beyond where the timber lies on the old photograph.

Little Inverey looking east (date uncertain)
The alder scrub on the banks of the Ey can be seen in the middle ground, while beyond, on the right, the wooded hill spur marks the site of 'New' Mar Lodge. The present Lodge, or its antecedent, would lie in direct line with the right-hand wooden box chimney of the thatched cottage. The rudimentary stock-pens and peat pile are noteworthy. Ground inspection suggests that it is highly likely that this photograph precedes the construction of the present Mar Lodge (completed 1898).

Braemar

The village of Braemar sits astride the River Clunie with the two geographically distinct 'sectors' of Castleton of Braemar on its eastern bank, built around the historical nucleus of Kindrochit Castle, Deeside stronghold of the Earl of Mar, and Auchendryne on its west bank. The twin sectors evolved in post-Culloden times under the aegis of their respective landowners and superiors; for Castleton, the Invercauld Farquharson's and for Auchendryne, the Earl of Fife (the Duff family). In the mid-eighteenth century, Braemar had a population of about two hundred and fifty, supported by a limited local agricultural base in pockets of lime-rich soils and good hill pastures. Historically, the animals were sent to the shealings, whose foundations abound in Glenshee and Glen Baddoch, thus releasing the valley bottomlands for grain production. Timber from the surviving pinewoods and grain in turn supported a suite of mills driven by the Clunie, as well as many smaller mills on the smaller tributary streams. Many of the now deserted clachans had their own corn kilns set into gravel mounds. By the early nineteenth century, the deer forest assets of Mar Forest were already advertised widely as the finest in Scotland. Sporting lets and the development of the sporting infrastructure in the form of roads, shooting lodges and bridges on the estates increased local employment opportunities and thus favoured expansion of village services and accommodation. The services provided included specialised professions such as the 'stuffers' (taxidermists), one of whom, John Lamont, operated from Mildarroch Cottage, just east of Inverey, and some of whose work may be seen in the Stag Ballroom at Mar Lodge. In addition to those visitors attracted to Braemar and its locality by angling, grouse and deer, the village established a Victorian reputation for the health-giving properties of its mountain air, and thus became, like Pitlochry, a fashionable up-market watering place and summer resort for families from the south.

By the 1890's, Braemar was described 'as a pretty town with well-built houses, all of which are slated, and a considerable number of excellent and beautiful villas' (Macintosh, 1898). The photographs which follow, however, reveal a fair number of low thatched cottages in the 1870's and 1880's, while by the 1890's the many timer-framed summer cottages and wooden gable-end extensions, which remain a feature of the village today, had already appeared. At the latter time, it was estimated that Braemar had a summer population of over two thousand 'living in it and its immediate surroundings' (Macintosh, 1898). The lodges welcomed house parties, and families, many from Aberdeen, took lets of houses for a part of the season, the owners often meanwhile retiring to their garden cottages. The twin estate superiority of Castleton and Auchendryne is manifested not only in the original provision of two separate Public Halls (the Jubille Hall – now the Invercauld Galleries – in Castleton, and the Victoria Hall in Auchendryne), but also in differences in feu-planning. The Castleton street pattern developed in a series of squares in contrast to the more relaxed positioning of Auchendryne, where the individual houses were often oriented to seek sun and view. The history of the Episcopal Church, initially of timber and eventually of stone, reflects the large numbers of English visitors attracted to the village from the 1880's until the 1930's, and their numbers are confirmed by the contemporary guidebooks listing accommodation and services. Towards the end of the nineteenth century, both the Invercauld and Fife Arms Hotels embarked on fairly ambitious extension schemes, and although Braemar did not achieve a rail link with Aberdeen, in the early twentieth century the Great North of Scotland Railway Company initiated a pioneering feeder omnibus service between Braemar and the Ballater railhead. The photographs of Braemar display an expanding late-Victorian village with a large summer and autumn visitor clientele to which both the village and estate infrastructures were closely geared.

Old Cottage on the Clunie below the Fife Arms and Clunie Mills

Braemar from Craig Coynach, c.1874

Particularly prominent are Braemar Parish Church and Manse (1870), St Andrew's Roman Catholic Chapel (1839), the original Braemar Parish Church (1830), now the Invercauld Festival Theatre, and the Fife Arms Stable Quadrangle (dated 1873). The original Parish Church was subsequently to be enhanced by a transept and spire (added in 1874), and both the Fife Arms and Invercauld Arms Hotels await their later extensions and, in the case of the former, its modern frontage. Many of the cottages in both Castleton and Auchendryne are thatched. The Easter Manse is shown in its original form, while the prominent mansions shown include Mayfield, Bellevue, Coldrach, Drumrunie, Geldie Cottage, Hilton, Woodside, Rowanlea, Mar Cottage and Sunnybrae. A familiar group in the Auchendryne Square beside the tailor's shop (now Haggart's Tweed Shop) includes Rose Cottage, Hayfield and Piedmont, but no Auchendryne Lodge. A large pile of stone at the rear of the Fife Arms Hotel appears to have been assembled for the hotel extension. Notable omissions include the two Public Halls, the Episcopal Church (in any form) and Braemar Lodge.

Braemar from Craig Coynach, c. 1897

Part of the key to dating this view is the existence of the wooden version of St. Margaret's Episcopal Church, initially erected in 1880 under the aegis of Bishop Suther of Aberdeen and Orkney to cater for English visitors to the village. The building shown includes the 1891 extension, also in wood, in the form of two transepts. As construction of the present stone church spanned the period 1898 - 1903, the photograph must have been taken between 1892 and 1897. The original parish church (Invercauld Festival Theatre) is shown with its 1874 extension. Major buildings appearing since the 1874 photograph include the Jubilee Hall (now the Invercauld Galleries), the Victoria Hall (lacking the later eastern extension), the Fife Arms Hotel extension, Morefield, Morrone Cottage, Braemar Lodge and Morven. A large number of wooden cottages have appeared in the village gardens, still a major feature of Braemar.

Braemar from Craig Coynach, c. 1903
St. Margaret's Episcopal Church has now been completed in stone (1903), while the Invercauld Extension and quadrangular steading is also completed. Other additions since 1897 include Morven Lodge and the Great North of Scotland Braemar Station for omnibuses.

Braemar from Craig Coynach in 1984

Site of present Braemar Games Ground, Auchendryne, c.1880
This view shows the lower end of Chapel Brae with the tailor's shop (Haggart's), Albany, Prospect Cottage and the three Broombank's, the latter forming the south-east arc of what is now the Princess Royal and Duke of Fife Memorial Park (1906). Auchendryne Lodge, Piedmont and St. Andrew's Catholic Church are also prominent buildings. The dating of this picture is from pictorial evidence not reproduced in this part of the original plate, notably the absence of the original version of St. Margaret's Episcopal Church. Also shown is the Invercauld Fountain (1870) and the original parish church (1874).

Part of Braemar prior to 1870
This damaged plate shows the present Braemar Parish Church (1870) under construction (no manse as yet), the pre-1874 'Invercauld Festival Theatre', and an unusual angle on the Clunie Mills. The large roof section to the right of the church and piles of timber suggest a measure of pre-assembly and fabrication, although the absence of heavy lifting gear appears to make this unlikely.

The Fife Arms Hotel, Braemar
The departure of the coach for Ballater with visitors, luggage and hotel staff provides a scene of considerable activity. The name of 'mine host', D. McNab, is prominently displayed above the main entrance. The abutment of the old Clunie bridge is visible in the foreground (still present).

Braemar in 1984

The Fife Arms Hotel, Braemar with its substantially re-modelled and heightened frontage
The completed stone version of St. Margaret's Episcopal Church which was completed in 1903 provides a chronological baseline for the picture.

The Invercauld Arms Hotel, Braemar

The photographer has captured the last phases in the construction of the eastern extension to the previously symmetrical Tudor-style building together with the arrival of the Great North of Scotland omnibuses, first introduced by the Company in May 1904 to link Ballater Railway Station with Braemar. The *Aberdeen Free Press* of 3rd May 1904 records the first run of these 'road motors' which were designed to accommodate sixteen passengers inside and a further two on the seat alongside the driver. The Milnes-Daimler omnibuses were equipped with cushioned seats and interior net racks, and the projecting canopy at each end of the vehicle provided cover for the conductor and driver. The initial twice daily return journey averaged one hour and thirty minutes, with the ascent of the hill west of Ballater past Craigendarroch being accomplished at around 5 miles per hour. During the first run, when the roads were described as "wet, stiff and claggy" and congested with "heavy holiday traffic" in the form of carriages, the upward journey took no less than one hour and forty five minutes. The Ballater-Braemar service, which terminated outside the Fife Arms Hotel, was the first of its kind to be introduced in Scotland, although similar vehicles had previously been successfully employed by the Great Western Railway Company.

Until 1910, the "road motors" had interchangeable bodies, the same chassis carrying a bus body in summer and lorry body in winter, when visitor traffic was substantially reduced. Thereafter, legislation insisted on vehicles being licensed for a single purpose. The omnibuses, which were subsequently extended on routes between Huntly and Aberchirder and Alford to Strathdon, formed important links in the famous 'Three Rivers Tour'. Initiated in June, 1907, this tour proved so popular that it survived into the days of L.N.E.R., and was frequently advertised on the front cover of the Great North of Scotland Railway's *Royal Route to the Highlands*, an annual tourist publication. For the convenience of passengers, the railway company operated a station and office behind the Invercauld Hotel, with adjacent garaging, waiting room and accommodation for the road motor agent. The building still stands and is the property of Northern Scottish. The main modifications to the Invercauld Arms are described in the 1886 *Royal Route to the Highlands* as being completed to designs by J. T. Wimperis Esq. of London, but the internal changes displayed in the photograph, with fairly massive timbers stacked outside, must post-date 1904 during the proprietorship of James Gregor.

The Clunie Mills, Braemar
This view of the Clunie mills immediately upstream of the road bridge looks towards Morrone and Tomintoul farm.

The Eastern approaches to Braemar
This view looks across the bridge over the mill lade for the lower Clunie Mills. The buildings featured have largely survived although the businesses are different. They are David Clark, General Merchant (described in the 1924 Guidebook as 'Grocer, Ironmonger, Clothier and General Merchant') who established his business in Castleton in 1881, and William Robb, "Jeweller to H.M. King George V as to King Edward VII", who ran a similar business in Ballater. A notice on the left announces "A Parade in Fancy Dress". Note the "claggy" state of the road, showing signs of the recent passage of both carriages and bicycles.

Braemar Castle (Mar Castle) with its annexe, now demolished

Invercauld House from the Lion's Face Rock, Braemar

The Braemar Gathering

Although historical accounts of Deeside emphasise the origins of the games as a medieval means of testing the fitness of retainers, strictly speaking the Braemar Royal Highland Society had its origins in the early nineteenth century in an annual procession and programme of social evenings initiated by a local group of carpenters and joiners. The traditional white aprons of the trade were worn during the procession which took place in July and was known as "The Wright's Walk". Under the Friendly Societies Act of 1816, and with the active encouragement of Farquharson of Monaltrie, the group was registered under the title "Braemar Wright's Friendly Society", with the laudable object of assisting the sick and aged amongst its members. The yearly subscription was four shillings, and the Society funds were invested in meal in response to the sequence of famine years which followed the year of the battle of Waterloo. The first clerk to the Society, appointed in 1821, was John Morgan, teacher at Auchendryne School (and latterly at Little Inverey). In the following year it was agreed that members should wear Highland dress at all meetings. The Earl of Fife became the first Honorary President to the Society in 1823.

In 1832, the first athletic competitions were held under Society auspices, and under the growing influence of the lairds, chiefly the Duke of Leeds who presented all his retainers with full Breadalbane Highland Dress, the neighbouring estates also turned out in full dress. In 1841, further competitions were inaugurated for reading and translating Gaelic. The venue of the games was peripatetic amongst the three major estates, the estate workers forming the principal competitors. In 1848, the year of Queen Victoria's first visit to Balmoral, when the games venue was Invercauld House, the date was postponed until early September to permit the Queen to attend, and in subsequent years, the Minutes of the Society reveal that the fixing of the date generally awaited the arrival of Her Majesty "into the country", that is, Deeside. In 1859, the Queen invited the Society to celebrate their games at Balmoral at her expense, and thus Balmoral was added to the list of Games venues which included the Cluny Park near the Old Invercauld Bridge, Invercauld House, Braemar Castle and Mar Lodge. No games were held in 1862 because of the death of Prince Albert, and it subsequently became customary not to hold gatherings in those years when a prominent personality connected with the event had died. In 1866, the title "Royal" was added to the Society's name.

In 1887, the year of the Golden Jubilee, Her Majesty again invited the Society to celebrate their games and gathering at Balmoral, entertaining the participants to luncheon on a grand scale. The site of these Balmoral Games was on the ground between the South Deeside Road and the Dee, now occupied by a part of Balmoral Golf Course. The Games and Royal Pavilion are illustrated in the accompanying photographs of the Balmoral Gathering in the year 1887. In the following year, there were no Games due to the death of Colonel J. F. Farquharson of Invercauld, while in 1889, the games were held at Mar Castle with the evening ball in the Victoria Hall, Auchendryne. Games were held at Mar Castle in the years 1893, 1894 and 1895, but none in the following two years, because of building operations at the present Mar Lodge. In 1898, the Gathering returned to Balmoral and the prize money was increased. In the following year, the competitions which had previously been restricted only to Society members were opened to members of the neighbouring Lonach Highland Society, foreshadowing the present largely open character of the events. In 1900, the Games were cancelled at the Queen's request as a mark of respect for the loss of life in the South African War, while in the following year the Society mourned the loss of its most enthusiastic Patron.

Subsequently, the Gathering, under the patronage of King Edward, centred itself in the Cluny Park near the present Invercauld Estate Office until in 1906, the Duke of Fife gave the Society twelve acres of ground in Auchendryne to create a permanent home for the Gathering, to be named "The Princess Royal Park". In that year, to help recoup outlay in preparing the ground, admission charges were set for the first time.

In the Gatherings which figure in the following pictures, one of the outstanding features was the march of the Clansmen – the Royal Highlanders from Balmoral wearing Stewart tartan, the Duff Highlanders from Mar, the Macduff tartan, and the Invercauld Highlanders wearing Farquharson tartan. The clansmen marched to the pipes and carried Lochaber battle axes, pikes and halberds. At the modern Gathering, the march of the Clansmen is replaced by the equally impressive march of the massed Pipe Bands. In 1971, the Braemar Royal Highland Society was assigned Ensigns Armorial by the Lord Lyon King at Arms, along with the dignity of being "taken, accounted and received as an Incorporation Noble within the Noblesse of Scotland". The Society motto – extremely appropriate in the light of its origins – is "For Kith and Kin".

The Royal Pavilion, Balmoral Gathering, 1887

In this year, the Games were held in the grounds of Balmoral at the invitation of H.M. Queen Victoria. In the picture, Her Majesty is accompanied by Princess Victoria of Wales and Princess Beatrice. The games became centralised in Braemar only from 1906. The Princess Royal whose name is incorporated together with her husband, the Duke of Fife, in the name of the Braemar Games Ground was Princess Louise, Queen Victoria's grand-daughter. The tradition of decorating the Royal Pavilion with heather and conifers continues to this day. The farm steading and Glebe cottage on the north side of the Dee (beside Old Crathie Kirk) can be picked out in the background, beyond the Royal Party.

The arrival of the Princess of Wales at the Balmoral Gathering
The year is almost certainly again 1887, and the building in the background is Crathie Manse. The ladies are carrying parasols rather than umbrellas, as many of the gentlemen are shading their eyes to catch a better sight of the Royal Arrival. The Guard of Honour comprises mainly Balmoral Highlanders (Lochaber axes and Royal Stewart tartan).

The Braemar Gathering at Mar Castle
The sequence of Games venues strongly suggests that this picture falls into the period 1983-95, when this was the Gathering Ground for three successive years.

The Braemar Games – dancing Ghillie-Callum

In this view, attention is concentrated on shot-putting rather than on the lone young dancer and his piper. The venue is again Balmoral. Ghillie-Callum or, as it is better known, the Sword Dance is regarded by the experts as probably the oldest of Highland dances, possibly dating back to the ninth century A.D. The popular story identifies its origins with a duel fought between Malcolm Canmore, King of Scots, and a noble follower of Macbeth. Having successfully disposed of his opponent, King Malcolm laid his adversary's sword on the ground, covered it with his own sword to create the form of a cross, and improvised a victory dance to the music of a harp. In sympathy with its alleged martial origins, this dance is performed with great verve and spirit. Highland Dancing, like many other aspects of Highland Society fell out of favour after Culloden, but regained the Royal seal of approval at the 1822 Royal Ball held in Holyrood, Edinburgh. Queen Victoria generally insisted on native Scottish dances being performed in her presence at Balmoral Court Balls, and her fiddler, Joseph Lowe, composed many reels to provide accompaniment.

BRAEMAR GATHERING. 10,386. G.W.W.

The Braemar Gathering at Balmoral

The Games are shown occupying the ground below the South Deeside Road at Crathie (now part of Balmoral Golf Course). Both the old and new Crathie Kirk sites are just cut off on the right. The ponies are tethered at the foot of the bank below the present road alignment. Note the use of carriages and traps as vantage points. It is almost certain that this is again the Balmoral venue of 1887, as the drapes in the Royal Pavilion are identical with a previous dated picture. Gatherings were also held on Balmoral ground in 1859, 1890, 1898 and 1899.

Crathie Church

The present Crathie church is the third of a sequence starting with the pre-Reformation kirk whose now roofless walls and churchyard stand beside the manse on the banks of the Dee. This church was in use until 1804, although the interior of the church, the vault and graveyard continues to be used for burials. The polished granite tombstones set up by H.M. Queen Victoria in memory of her retainers at Balmoral are of particular interest to visitors. A second church, shown in the accompanying photograph, was built in 1804 on the site of the present Crathie church. It was a plain building with a small belfry, its internal austerity being relieved only by two windows on either side of the pulpit installed by Queen Victoria in memory of Dr Norman Macleod. The last service in this church took place on 23rd April, 1893.

The present church stands exactly on the same site. The square tower which figures prominently in the photograph rising above the intersection of the nave and transepts, sits on arches which rest on granite pillars, The main door is in the west gable, while the south transept is set aside for the Royal Family. The cost of building was raised by a combination of private donations together with the £2400 raised in a two-day Bazaar (see the splendid Bazaar book entitled *Under Lochnagar*). Princesses and Duchesses were numbered amongst the stallholders and Queen Victoria visited the bazaar on no less than five occasions. The Great North of Scotland Railway Company ran special excursion services from Aberdeen to the Bazaar, and its success permitted the opening and dedication of the new Crathie Church on 18th June, 1895.

In contrast to its predecessor, the church interior is richly decorated with stained glass windows and memorials presented by members of the Royal Family. The granite pulpit carries pillars made up of fifteen varieties of Scottish granites. The stained glass window in the south transept was installed by H.M. Queen Victoria principally in memory of her mother, Victoria, Duchess of Kent, but other members of her family commemorated are her youngest son, Prince Leopold (1853-1884), her son-in-law, Prince Frederick William (later Emperor) of Prussia (1831-1888), her husband Prince Albert, the Prince Consort (1819-1861), her second daughter Princess Alice, Grand Duchess of Hesse (1843-1878) and Prince Louis, Grand Duke of Hesse (1837-1892).

Crathie, about 1890

This view looks across the haughs of the Dee valley from the terrace edge immediately above the South Deeside Road. The hill in the background is Creag a' Chlamhain. The foreground is now occupied by a part of the Balmoral Golf Course. On the far bank of the Dee stands the manse and Old Crathie Churchyard, while beyond, standing above the line of the modern North Deeside Road, and near the line of the old Deeside Road, occupying the same site as the present Crathie Church, is its rather simpler predecessor (1804-1893). West of this church, the Post Office building and old schoolhouse (Highcliff) can be picked out amongst the trees. The trees in the foreground were almost certainly planted at the time of the unveiling of the Prince Consort's statue (1867) but have subsequently been felled and the copse replanted at the time of the laying out of the golf course. The photograph pre-dates the building of the United Free Church (1896) and manse. The bazaar to raise funds for the construction of the present Crathie Church (foundation stone laid September, 1893) was held in the field in the foreground in September, 1894, and the present church completed in the following year. A comparative view in 1984 is shown on the right.

Crathie Church in the late 1890's

This photograph was almost certainly taken shortly after the opening of the modern church in 1895, and looks towards the gap in the wooded bank which was the site of the previous view (just to the left of the church spire). Left again, in the trees, is the cluster of houses and the shop of Easter Balmoral (named Crathie on the 1903 edition of the Ordnance Survey map). On the extreme left, the road leads to the suspension bridge (1834), passing the Public Hall (1895) with the flagstaff. To the right of the church is Baile-na-coille, and right again, the Dairy. The Public Hall (or Old Hall as it is locally termed) was originally built behind the old Crathie Schoolhouse (Highcliff) to accommodate the congregation while the present Crathie Church was being built. It was then shifted and re-erected on the site shown here and served a variety of community uses until burnt down on 14th March, 1981. Its successor lies near Easter Balmoral. The original Crathie Post Office (or 'Letter Receiving House'), was built in the 1840's with trading done through the cottage window. The eastern gable, which until recently served as the Post Office was built on at the request of Queen Victoria, who persuaded the family who operated it (and who still live in the house) to settle in Crathie. There have been a number of minor additions and modifications to the tower of the church since this picture was taken, but the most notable was the addition of an eastern vestry donated by H.M. The Queen Mother in 1956.

Balmoral

In the first eight years of their marriage, Victoria and Albert made three visits to Scotland. These visits excited considerable interest as with the exception of George IV's short stay in Edinburgh in 1822, no British monarch had stayed in Scotland since the days of Charles II. The Royal couple made the decision to seek a home in the Highlands for regular holidays in the autumn and the location was at least partially decided on health grounds. The Queen's physician, Sir James Clark, was regarded as an authority on the influence of climate on health, and his own son, John, was at the time convalescing on Deeside. He visited Sir Robert Gordon at Balmoral, and identified the locality as one of pure air and ample sunshine, at least by comparison with the West Highlands where the Queen had experienced wet weather. The sudden death of Sir Robert left the lease of Balmoral free, and Prince Albert sought weather reports on Deeside and obtained, through the good offices of the Earl of Aberdeen, three water colours of the castle executed by the landscape architect, Woodside-born James Giles, designer of Haddo House gardens. Since the start of his lease from the Earl of Fife, Sir Robert made extensive re-building and re-construction to the original tower keep, producing a rather rambling picturesque building in the Scottish baronial style. In 1848, Queen Victoria instructed her solicitors to acquire the lease on her husband's behalf, and by 1852, the Balmoral Estate Act enabled Prince Albert to acquire the Balmoral freehold from the Fife Trustees for the sum of 30,000 guineas. The initial Royal visit to Balmoral, involving a triumphal journey up Deeside is described in the *Aberdeen Journal* of September 13th, 1848, and illustrated by sketches in the pages of the *Illustrated London News*.

However, Sir Robert's Balmoral was too small and cramped for a growing Royal family which brought with it guests, court members, politicians and retainers, and Aberdeen architect William Smith was engaged to design a bigger castle, to be built almost on the same site, of white granite, with Scottish baronial-style turrets. Prince Albert's Balmoral was set within landscaped grounds, with poplars and pines introduced from his native Coburg. Inside, the decor was almost exclusively Scottish, with carpets, curtains and upholstery of Royal Stuart and green Hunting Stuart tartans, and walls hung with Highland weapons, trophies and Landseer paintings. Important Royal and national events, including funerals and marriages or engagements were commemorated on the Balmoral skylines in the form of monuments, and the Royal couple embarked on expeditions exploring the surrounding countryside. In her later life, Queen Victoria spent about four months in each year at Balmoral, and received politicians, including Gladstone and Disraeli. Ministers, guests and dispatches travelled to Balmoral by special train. George Washington Wilson was engaged to record the building and interior decoration of Balmoral by Prince Albert, and this Royal patronage did much to establish the early part of his photographic career.

Birkhall, Glen Muick

The original house of Birkhall was built in 1715 by Captain Charles Gordon of Minmore and his wife, Rachel Gordon, tenth laird of Abergeldie. The ninth laird, John Gordon, left no family, hence the marriage of his sister Rachel to Captain Gordon retained the name Gordon in the line. Their eldest son, Peter, became the eleventh laird of Abergeldie, and their third son, Joseph, a prominent Jacobite, lived at Birkhall. In 1848, the fifteenth laird of Abergeldie, Michael Francis Gordon, rented Abergeldie to Queen Victoria, and in 1852, Prince Albert purchased Birkhall, intending it as the Scottish home of his eldest son, the Prince of Wales, later Edward VII. In fact, Edward only stayed at Birkhall on one occasion – in 1862, the year before his marriage to Princess Alexandra of Denmark – and in 1885, Birkhall passed to his mother, thus effectively becoming a part of the Balmoral property. In the late 1880's, an extension wing and entrance porch was added (shown in this photograph), followed by an annex. The house was frequently "lent" to other members of the Royal family and to distinguished visitors. Included amongst the latter were Sir James Clark, the Queen's Physician, Florence Nightingale, Lord Panmure and the geologist, Sir Charles Lyell. In 1957, Her Majesty The Queen Mother initiated a restorative and extension scheme at Birkhall involving two new wings to blend with the 18th century mansion. The same blue-grey slates from Meall Dubh (The Black Hill) were used in the extension as on the original house.

A winter scene at Balmoral amongst the birches

The Balmoral lands belonged historically to a branch of the Abergeldie Gordons, and subsequently to the Farquharson's of Inverey. In 1798, the estate became the property of the earl of Fife. The last in a succession of lease-holders was Sir Robert Gordon, brother of Lord Aberdeen, and for some years ambassador at the Hapsburg court. On Sir Robert's death in 1847, Prince Albert secured the remainder of the castle lease, thus beginning the long royal connection with Balmoral. Sir Robert's Balmoral Castle was first visited by Queen Victoria in September, 1848. It was described by Prince Albert as "a little castle of granite with numerous small turrets and white-washed" (i.e. harled). In 1852, Albert converted his lease into ownership of castle and estate, and on September 28th, 1853, Her Majesty laid the foundation stone of the present building.

Baile na Coille, Balmoral
This house was built by Queen Victoria for her favourite retainer John Brown, and now acts as the home of the Queen's Resident
Factor for the Balmoral Estates.

Alltnaguibhsaich, Glen Muick

Originating as a "sod-covered one-chimneyed building" for a deer watcher, Alltnaguibhsaich first developed into "a most commodious cottage belonging to Captain Gordon of Abergeldie" (McConnochie, 1898). The cottage was described by Queen Victoria in her *Journal* as "our humble little abode" or simply "The Hut", but by 1849 had been expanded by the construction of a second building. The original, shown in this picture, retains its sod roof. The accommodation, described in Queen Victoria's *Journal,* consisted of dining room, sitting room, bedroom and dressing room, maid's room and little pantry, while in the other building (on the left of the photograph), was a kitchen "where people generally sit", the servant's dining room, a store room, with a loft above "for sleeping the menfolk". By the time McConnochie had published his picture book *Views of Royal Deeside,* c.1905, the second (left hand) building shown here had been heightened to create a second storey, a porch added, and further connected outbuildings had been constructed at the rear. The picture here thus represents a phase in the lodge's history between "the little bothie" and its early twentieth century form.

Glassalt Shiel, Lock Muick

As with Alltnaguibhsaich, this building was originally a very small shiel (see picture dated 1862 in Clark's *Balmoral – Queen Victoria's Highland Home).* This locality, magnificently situated below the Glas Allt falls on the shores of the loch, was a favourite with the Prince Consort. It was in response to his liking that Queen Victoria built her "Widow's house" there in 1868, "at this favourite wild spot". The house warming is described in her *Journal* (October 1st, 1868). The totally new house shown here replaced Alltnaguibhsaich in her affections. Described by Queen Victoria as "a compact little house", there were six rooms upstairs and, on the ground floor, a sitting room, bedroom, maid's room, hall, dining room, kitchen, steward's room and manservant's room. The stables and keeper's cottage, also shown in this picture, lay at the rear, the latter serving as accommodation for the gillies. As with Alltnaguibhsaich, the Glassalt Shiel was connected to Bamoral by a substantially built and well-graded carriage road.

Ballater

Ballater had its origins as a small clachan named Ballaver on the extensive terrace flanking Craigendarroch known significantly as "The Muir". The medieval settlement lay one mile eastwards on the well drained fan of the Burn of Tullich, clustered around the ancient parish church of Tullich. However, in 1800, the post-Culloden initiatives in Highland estate management led to the creation of a new planned village being promoted on "The Muir" around a new centrally located church built in 1798. The local laird, Francis Farquharson of Monaltrie had been an enthusiastic supporter of the young Pretender, and was factor to his uncle's estates at Invercauld. He led three hundred Invercauld clansmen to Culloden and was subsequently to have his estate of Monaltrie forfeited and to suffer imprisonment in the Tower of London. However, Francis eventually secured a pardon, married a Derbyshire lady of means, and returned to his restored estate where he began a programme of estate improvement and promotion of the mineral springs of Pannanich. These springs had been known since at least the early eighteenth century and were already attracting sufferers to the neighbourhood, the waters being described as "a stimulant, a tonic and agreeable to the taste".

Farquharson built comfortable accommodation at Pannanich including an octagon "for the better sort to retire to". He laid out the Muir for feus in a grid pattern and built connecting roads between Ballater and the springs. As Tullich declined, so the growth of Ballater as a spa village led to demand for a bridge across the Dee. In 1783, the first bridge was completed, the money being mainly raised by public subscription topped up by a grant from the Forfeited Estates Commission. This bridge survived until 1799 when it was swept away by an August flash flood, one year after the new central church with its timber spire was constructed. The replacement bridge, which was Telford-designed, was completed in 1809, but was swept away by the muckle spate of 1829. The replacement bridge, which was a timber structure resting on granite foundations and which figures in the accompanying photographs of Ballater, was completed in 1834 and remained in use until 1884. During the lifetime of this timber bridge, the feus on the Muir filled up with granite villas and slated cottages, the early areas of development lying in the vicinity of the bridge and Monaltrie (now the Invercauld) Hotel. Thatched cottages and timber buildings were translated into slate and stone, and the village "became much frequented in summer by strangers from a distance on account of the salubrity of the air and the beauty of the scenery" (*New Statistical Account,* 1841). In the early days of the timber-spired church, the minister newly appointed nearly lost his post because he could not speak the Gaelic! On 17th October, 1866, the Deeside Railway reached Ballater, permitting visitors to travel by train rather than by coach. In 1873, the original United church was demolished and replaced one year later by the present church. Other prominent Victorian additions to the Ballater skyline, shown in the photographs, include the Barracks, the Albert Memorial Hall and the string of mansions along the flanks of Craigendarroch. In 1886, Ballater railway station was rebuilt to include a roof erected over a part of the platform, while a large shed was also erected for "garaging" the Royal carriages while the Queen was in residence in Balmoral. By the time that the present bridge was erected in 1885, Ballater's present recreational and service role had been firmly established.

Ballater from the south, 1868

This early view repays comparison with a view reproduced in Fraser's *The Old Deeside Road* (1921) dated 1856. The George Washington Wilson view shows the Square set out in feus, and largely infilled with slated houses, save for a few on the south side of Hawthorn Place and Victoria Road. The Square is dominated by the Old Parish Church of Ballater (1798-1872). The road to the old Dee ford just upstream of the timber bridge (1834-1885) is clearly shown, while the adjacent steading, which does not appear in Fraser's view, is completed. Note the cornricks and founs, and the group of pre-Victorian houses clustered in the vicinity of the bridge. The original Monaltrie Arms has already been replaced by the Invercauld Arms (c.1860), and the Victoria Barracks (1860) appear in the top left of the photograph. Just beyond can be seen the line of the embankment designed for the railway or tramway extension (for goods only) running from Ballater Station (1866) to Balgairn Farm, just beyond the Gairn. As this extension is clearly shown as being under construction, and as operations on it ceased in 1868 when the entrepreneur James Ross Farquharson of Invercauld leased Ballochbuie Forest to Queen Victoria, it may be surmised that the photograph dates from 1867-68.

Ballater from the south-east, c.1890

The photograph post-dates the construction of the 1885 granite bridge. The granite bases for the previous wooden bridge can be seen (as today) just downstream in the river bed. Since the 1868 picture, there has been considerable infill and extension of feus, notably to the west of the Square, while prominent near the railway station is the Albert Memorial Hall (1875). The Gordon Institute and Victoria Hall (both 1895) are missing. The Darroch Learg (1880) and Oakhill (1890) are shown, while the Invercauld Arms displays its Tudor extension on the riverside. The Parish Church in the Square built to plans by Aberdeen architect J. Russel Mackenzie in 1873-74, and replacing the 1798 "church on the moor", can be clearly seen, while on the bottom left, on the riverside, there are logs which may have been floated down the Dee. The tip of the re-built railway station (1886) is shown, but the corner block at the south-east of Ballater Square (1906) is missing. On that basis, the picture is dated c.1890.

Ballater in the days of the 1834 timber bridge
This bridge, built of local timber, consisted of four arches. It survived until 1885, when the present bridge was opened by Queen Victoria. The 1834 bridge was built by the Aberdeen firm, Gibb of Rubislaw, to plans approved by Thomas Telford. The 1873 Ballater Parish Church is prominent, but the Albert Memorial Hall (1875), which might have made dating more accurate, would have been concealed by the Invercauld Arms Hotel.

The Albert Memorial Hall, Ballater, 1874.
The photographer here records the building almost completed, although the inscription to Prince Albert has not yet been fitted. The inscription was to read "A Prince indeed, and above all titles, a Household Word – hereafter through all time, Albert the Good". The celebration of the opening of the Ballater Bridge by H.M. Queen Victoria in 1885, for which deputations from Deeside and Aberdeen were assembled in Ballater by special train, centred on a concert and ball in this hall.

Ballater in the 1890's

For comparison, this post-1885 view from approximately the same point, displays the Invercauld Arms with its Tudor extension, with the Albert Memorial Hall just visible over the hotel ridge-line. Railway carriages may be seen in the station sidings, together with considerable quantities of smoke and steam.

Ballater in 1984

Charleston of Aboyne

Aboyne, centred around its extensive green, was the creation of the first Earl of Aboyne who in 1660 married Margaret Irvine of Drum, and ten years later promoted a burgh of barony charter for a village to be built on a greenfield site half a mile distant from Aboyne Castle. The green was envisaged as the site for the weekly agricultural market. By the 1690's, the Aberdeenshire Poll Book records a merchant, four weavers, one tradesman and two shoemakers as resident in Charleston of Aboyne. With the growth of this new nucleation, the old settlement east of the present Loch of Aboyne at Formaston-Kirkton gradually declined. The Mains farm of the castle became the centre of agricultural improvements, chiefly the enclosure of the fields by stone dykes, the skilled labour for their construction being imported from Angus. Aboyne Castle was greatly extended by the addition of substantial wings in 1801 and 1869, and its policies enhanced by woodland and the creation of the entirely artificial Loch of Aboyne in 1834. The creation of new water bodies was a feature of estate management in the nineteenth century and another example – Birsemore – appears in the general view of Aboyne, having been created partly for amenity and fish stocking, and partly to drive sawmills.

In 1888, the by now very substantial and composite building of Aboyne Castle was bought by Sir William Cunliffe Brooks, whose daughter Amy married the eleventh Marquis of Huntly. Brooks, who was a Manchester banker by profession, also purchased the Glen Tanar estate. In the 'nineties, he exercised his ideas of landscape architecture both on Glen Tanar and in the village of Aboyne (see Charleston Cottages in the Station Square), and the rebuilt station buildings at Aboyne appear to have been designed to accord with his ideas. Much of the contemporary character of both Glen and village, including the Fungle with its inscribed stone mottoes, are a product of one man's perception of landscape architecture.

Aboyne and its surroundings from the south-west
This view, taken from Parkside on the Fungle, looks across the two artificial water bodies in the mid-ground (see boat house on left shore of the larger), towards Aboyne Green. Familiar landmarks include Old Aboyne Station, the Loch of Aboyne, Birse Lodge, Aboyne Castle, and the old suspension bridge across the Dee (demolished and replaced by the present structure in 1941). The suspension bridge was erected in 1871, and at its northern end stood the old Boat Inn (Bridge-end Inn) which is shown here in its original form of a long composite thatched house consisting of stables, dwelling house and byre. On the skyline, the pattern of rotationally burnt grouse moors on Mortlich are prominent. The railway embankment and mill which figure in a later picture, together with the bridge over the Tarland Burn can be picked out on the extreme right mid-ground.

Old Cottage at Aboyne

The spire of the Free, subsequently United Free Church is visible immediately to the left of the cottage gable, together with the Birsemore water body. This cottage, sited at Parkside, can be picked out on the bottom left of the previous photograph, and sits on the approaches to the Fungle.

The eastern approaches to Aboyne in the 1890's

This photograph pre-dates the reconstruction of the station buildings and square in the 1890's. The railway embankment in the foreground crosses by a stone bridge (abutment used by present footbridge) the waters of the Tarland Burn which drove the corn and flour mill seen in the left foreground. Adjacent stands the sawmill, while left of centre, the railway water cistern. The "roundhouse", in direct line with St. Machar's Parish Church, remains a summer house in the grounds of the Huntly Arms, while the school on the Green (1875) displays its 1890 extension, but not a further extension dating from 1901 (now the Aboyne Business Centre).

Aboyne Station Square, c.1900
As with Banchory, Aboyne Station was rebuilt in the early 1900's with an imposing facade, possibly influenced by Cunliffe Brooks' ideas on architecture which appear to be reflected in many of Aboyne's later buildings, for example, Charleston Cottages on Station Square.

Glen Tanar House
As originally built in the 1890's by Sir William Cunliffe Brooks, a Manchester banker, and owner of the Glen Tanar Estate.

Aboyne Castle and its policies

Prominent on the skyline is the Earl of Aboyne's Memorial obelisk on Mortlich which collapsed in 1912. In recent years, the Victorian additions to the castle have been demolished. Only the orignal tower house block is retained.

The Burn of Vat, Dinnet

This spectacular glacial meltwater-carved pothole, known to Victorian guidebooks as Gilderoy's Cave, here displays its Victorian grafitti, the dates spanning the period 1871-1875. Gilderoy is reputed to have been a member of the clan MacGregor, a group of whom settled in 17th century middle Deeside, who earned his living by raiding. He has been wrongly confused with Rob Roy MacGregor. Gilderoy regarded the Vat as his most comfortable retreat. He was eventually hung for his crimes in 1639.

At a curling bonspiel, Loch of Aboyne

This artificial loch, created in 1834 to enhance the policies of Aboyne Castle, was frequently the scene of curling bonspiels. Indeed, so popular were these bonspiels that in the 'nineties the railway ran special excursions from Aberdeen to a temporary stop beside the Loch.

Loch Kinord, Dinnet

This photograph was taken at the point where the Nature Conservancy Council has recently erected a viewpoint on their Burn of Vat trail. It looks across the smallholding (latterly the tearoom, and at present the Warden's Office), towards Castle Island and Loch Kinord. As the following contemporary view shows, there have been major changes in land use in the foreground, with most of the fields now reverted to moorland or birch scrub. Note the horse and trap on the Tarland road in the left centre.

Loch Kinord, Dinnet, in 1984

Banchory

The present settlement of Banchory evolved from two historically distinct nuclei. At the east was the ancient kirkton, often known as the Townhead, sitting above the old kirkyard, and dominated by the "new kirk" (1824), built along the line of the Aberdeen turnpike. In 1841, the *New Statistical Account* described the kirkton as consisting of "the old manse, two endowed schools, eight labourer's cottages, and a farmhouse with steading". However nineteenth century growth was to concentrate on a new site further west at Arbeadie, and by the time of the same *New Statistical Account,* Arbeadie, strung out along the line of the High Street, boasted fifty houses, a population of three hundred and fifty, and the dignity of burgh of barony. The village had a Post Office, Episcopal Church (1851), two schools, a branch of the Bank of Scotland and no less than three inns. A number of Banchory's inhabitants were then associated with the timber trade, including the floating of timber rafts down the Dee to Aberdeen, a business which remained a familiar sight on the Dee at the time the Deeside Railway reached the village in 1853.

Writing in 1860, James Brown described Banchory as having become "the abode of divers gentlemen, both from Aberdeen and other parts". He continued "there are more gentlemen's houses in and near Banchory than in any other village near Aberdeen . . . these houses being all ornamented with gardens, lawns and gravel walks". He also claimed that Banchory was "much resorted to during the summer by persons of weak health". The photographs of Banchory in the late Victorian period which follow depict a settlement which already had a population of nearly fifteen hundred, and which boasted a Town Hall (1872) and the prominent West Church (1885). By the time the Burnett Public Park had been opened in 1887, Banchory's services and shops not only reflected its resident and summer-time population and its weekend visitors from Aberdeen, but also its rich agricultural hinterland. As with Lumphanan and Torphins, the railway played an important role in its prosperity. In Banchory's case, the Station Buildings were impressively rebuilt in stone in 1902.

Banchory Ternan in the 1870s'.

Lumphanan in the 1890's

Prominent in this view are the Stohert Memorial Church and Manse (1870), the Macbeth Arms and adjoining shop (1860), and the old bank. Opposite the Parish Hall (with flagstaff and miniature spire), stands the Merchant's Post Office. The Hall is dated 1897. The railway station which attracted growth away from nearby Old Lumphanan and Burnside village is also shown.

Lumphanan in 1984

The Square, Torphins, in the late 1890's

As the contemporary view which follows reveals, the range of services offered in the smaller Aberdeenshire villages has declined since the advent of the motor car. In this view are saddler, shoemaker, chemist and cycle shop. The hairdresser on the right is advertising Mitchell's XXX Bogie Roll, and the newspaper boards announce "A Royal Betrothal" – probably the engagement of George V to Queen Mary of Teck. The fountain in the foreground commemorates the sixtieth year of "Queen Victoria's beneficent reign" and was erected by public subscription in 1897.

The Square, Torphins, in 1984

Banchory High Street

This view, from the number of plates surviving in the University Collection, was a favourite. It illustrates the changes taking place in the last thirty years of the nineteenth century in the High Street, both in the proprietors and in the style of the shop frontages. The later view shows the then site of Banchory Post Office (extreme right), while Alexander Lunan (Chemist) has acquired a second Druggist's emblem. Note the form of street lighting and the kerbside standpump, with handy bracket to rest your bucket.

Banchory High Street in the 1890's
The picture is dominated by Banchory West Church (1885), the original Burnett Arms and the range of houses beginning to undergo frontal conversion into shops on their ground floors. On the left, the Banchory Hotel advertises stabling, while the deep gutters carry mobile duckboards. The railway bridge is visible in the distance.

The Western end of Banchory High Street
The premises of George Beattie – Saddler and Harness Maker – are conveniently located opposite the Banchory Hotel Stables.

Banchory Ternan from the south
Behind the landmark of the railway embankment can be picked out (from left to right), Corsee House, the Town Hall (1872), Windsor House, the beginnings of Ramsay Road, Ravenswood and Summerhill, Bellfield House and Castle Airy.

Banchory Golf Course

Cults

The accompanying photographs reveal the gradual growth of suburbia along the North Deeside Road in the last twenty years of the nineteenth century, with a progressive invasion of the countryside by the merchant families of Aberdeen, encouraged by the station at Cults and eventually, in 1894, by the Deeside Suburban rail service which established stations at Pitfodels and West Cults, followed by Bieldside in 1897. The line was double-tracked in 1899. Macintosh (1895) notes that "the greater parts of the Lands of Pitfodels is now studded with beautiful mansions and villas, each of which stands amid well-laid out and carefully kept grounds. They mostly belong to manufacturers and gentlemen engaged in business in Aberdeen and retired gentlemen". He adds that "the suburban village of Cults has rapidly extended in recent years. It stands on a fine situation with a southern exposure. The villas and cottages are neat and clean and present the features of convenience and comfort. A considerable number of excellent dwelling houses have been erected on both sides of the line in the vicinity of the station".

The mansions stand amidst an earlier pattern of fields and farm steadings which survive today in terms of drystone dykes and place names. Key buildings in the dating, apart from the houses themselves, are the original Free Church in Kirk Brae (1843), its Manse (1863), Cults West Church (Hall 1883, Church 1916), Cults East Church (1903) and West Cults Station (1894).

Cults Station c.1900

This picture recalls the days of the "subbies" on the Deeside Line inaugurated between Aberdeen and Culter in 1894 and passing, as the contemporary newspaper accounts expressed it, "the lavish homes of the city's merchant princes". The time on the station clock is twenty minutes past one, and the up-train passengers are crossing the footbridge to have their tickets checked at the station gate. On the Deeside line, there were local stations at Ruthrieston, Pitfodels, West Cults, Bieldside, Murtle and Milltimber. On the line today, many of the station buildings survive as private houses and workshops, now passed by walkers and joggers. Services were finally withdrawn in April, 1937, leaving behind a record of fifty years punctual and efficient service, epitomised by the number of passengers leaving the station while the up-train was already on its way to West Cults station.

Cults from the south.

This view looks across the "Shakking Briggie" to the old Engine House of the Aberdeen Waterworks (now Fairview) with, adjacent, St. Devenick Cottage and Loirsbank. On the left midground, the old Free Church and manse appear on Kirk Brae, while Abbotsville occupies its prominent site just to the east of Cults Square. From left to right, just below the horizon, isolated houses include Craigton, Morkeu and Cliff House, while bisecting a line linking the old Engine House with Morkeu stands Mayfield House, Birchfield and Ashfield Villas. Westerton Drive is completed, but only Abbotshill Cottage is built on the northern margin of the North Deeside Road. Other mansions shown include Wellwood, Woodlands, Arnlee, Fushiabank, Inverey, Craigmount, Inverdee and Westerton of Pitfodels.

Cults from the south in 1984

West Cults about 1880

Prominent on the skyline, just left of centre, is the Bieldside Cairn, with, to the east, Hillhead Farm and the steading of Mains of Cults. East of the Bieldside House policies, on the far side of the North Deeside Road, stand the cornricks of Gateside Farm. The view pre-dates 1883-4, as the mansion of Ingleside first appears in the Suburban section of the Aberdeen *Post Office Directory* for that year. West Cults Farmhouse is also missing, although the approach road to the present farmhouse, which was constructed for gravel extraction and access to the old Cults tip, is·shown.

West Cults in 1984